LEADING FOR GOOD

The New Executive Director's Blueprint to Leading and Sustaining a Thriving Nonprofit

DR. TAMARA W. DIAS

ISBN: 979-8-9924324-1-1 (Paperback)
ISBN: 979-8-9924324-0-4 (eBook)
Library of Congress Control Number: 2025900850

Because of the dynamic nature of the internet, any web addresses or links contained in this book may have changed since publication and may no longer be valid. The views expressed in this work are solely those of the author and do not necessarily reflect the views of the publisher, and the publisher disclaims any responsibility for them.

Printed in the United States of America

For every nonprofit leader who wants to do good work and leave the world better than they found it. Trust the process, because you are making a difference.

Visit www.myleadershipbook.com
For free resources to help you lead
with confidence and clarity.

TABLE OF CONTENTS

INTRODUCTION

Thank you for picking up this book. If you're reading this, it's because you care deeply about making a difference as a nonprofit leader. You believe in the mission of your organization and the impact it can have on the world. But let's be honest—this work is far from easy. Balancing limited resources with ambitious goals, supporting a team while keeping donors engaged, and somehow finding time for yourself? It can often feel overwhelming.

I understand how heavy that responsibility can feel because I've carried it, too. When I first stepped into nonprofit leadership, I was excited, determined, and perhaps a bit naïve. I believed my passion for the mission would be enough to carry me through the inevitable challenges. What I didn't anticipate was the relentless pressure—financial constraints, difficult board meetings, staff turnover, and the nonstop pace of it all. There were moments when I doubted myself and felt I was failing the very people I set out to serve. And there were countless moments of disappointment—when grant funding fell through or when a donor shifted their priorities.

Maybe you've experienced something similar. Maybe you've questioned whether you're truly cut out for this work. Perhaps you've spent sleepless nights trying to figure out how to stretch your budget, repair team dynamics, or simply make it to the following week.

Perhaps you've found yourself staring at a growing inbox and a dwindling operating budget. You're not alone. Many nonprofit leaders wrestle with these same challenges, but here's the good news: there's a way forward.

I wrote this book because I've walked in your shoes. I've learned—sometimes the hard way—what it takes to lead with confidence, clarity, and purpose. While I've faced significant challenges, I've also had incredible wins. This isn't a collection of abstract theories or feel-good advice; it's a practical guide designed to help you navigate the real-world challenges of nonprofit leadership. Together, we'll explore key areas such as financial literacy, team dynamics, donor relationships, and self-care. Throughout the book, I'll share stories and lessons from my own journey so you know you're not alone in facing these obstacles.

Before we dive into strategies and solutions, I'd like to share a bit more about my journey. My path to leadership wasn't linear, nor was it smooth. There were moments of doubt, but there were also breakthroughs—times when I realized that my struggles weren't merely obstacles but opportunities for growth.

When I stepped into my first leadership role, I thought success would be the natural result of hard work and a clear vision. I believed that if I simply worked hard enough, everything would fall into place. While hard work and vision certainly played a role, they weren't enough. I quickly learned that nonprofit leadership demands more than passion—it requires the ability to navigate complex, often uncharted, terrain. It means balancing the needs of your community with the harsh realities of limited resources, motivating your team even when you feel drained, and staying laser-focused on your mission despite the weight of it all.

I vividly remember one particularly difficult year when everything seemed to unravel at once. Donations were down, team morale was low, and a key community partnership was on the brink of collapse. I spent countless nights agonizing over decisions, questioning every move. The pressure to solve every problem felt insurmountable. But during that period of struggle, I had a crucial realization: leadership isn't about having all the answers—it's about asking the right questions, trusting your team, and staying anchored in your values.

That shift in perspective changed everything for me. I began approaching leadership with a renewed focus on sustainability, collaboration, and continuous growth rather than perfection. I started viewing challenges as opportunities to innovate rather than as failures to be feared. I leaned into partnerships—both within my organization and across the community—and learned the importance of setting boundaries to show up as the best version of myself.

This book is the result of those hard-earned lessons. It's a guide for leaders who want to lead with purpose and resilience and overcome obstacles without losing themselves in the process. Whether you're navigating your first year as a nonprofit leader or a seasoned executive looking for fresh insights, this book is for you.

I won't promise an easy road—because there is no such thing in this work. But I can promise you this: you are not alone. The challenges you face are shared by leaders across the world, and they are solvable. You have what it takes to lead with confidence, inspire your team, and create lasting change. All it requires is a willingness to learn, adapt, and keep going.

If you've ever felt overwhelmed, uncertain, or stuck, this book is for you. My hope is that it will provide you with the tools and encouragement you need to persevere, to lead effectively, and to make the impact you were meant to make.

As you turn the page and dive into the first chapter, know that you've already taken a powerful first step—you've chosen to invest in yourself as a leader. You've sought out the strategies and tools that will help you not just survive but thrive. Most importantly, you've chosen to believe in your ability to make a difference.

I'm honored to join you on this journey.

PART 1

Building a Strong Foundation

Success is built on a foundation of clarity, knowledge, and intention. When you understand where you stand, you can confidently chart the course ahead."

Visit www.myleadershipbook.com to download the Organizational SWOT Analysis.

CHAPTER 1

Understand Your Ecosystem

" *Success begins with knowing the landscape. A well-tended ecosystem is the foundation for growth."*

"Welcome. Now, go raise us some money!"

Those were the first words spoken to me by the Vice Chairperson of the Board of Directors of the nonprofit organization I had just begun leading. They handed me a laptop and the keys to the office and, with a pat on the back, gave me the charge to secure the funding needed to sustain the organization. While I managed to keep a smile on my face, it didn't match the butterflies in my stomach and the sudden wave of nausea that hit me as reality set in. I was officially in charge—with full responsibility not just to manage the organization's current assets but also to set a vision for its future.

As the Vice Chairperson walked to their car and drove away, I sat in my office chair, staring at the empty walls around me. "This is it," I thought. Taking a deep breath, I opened the laptop to check my newly created email account, which—at least for that moment—still had zero emails (a rare and fleeting moment, as I soon learned). I spent most of that day reviewing the 90-day goals I had outlined during my final interview with the

Board of Directors a few weeks earlier. However, it quickly became clear that I needed more than just my initial plan if I wanted to succeed. I needed context. I needed to understand what had come before me, what the organization's most pressing issues were, and where opportunities lay. In short, I needed conversations.

Becoming an Executive Director was the first role where I felt equal parts excitement and pressure. On one hand, I felt the weight of my new title and the responsibility it carried. On the other, I was thrilled by the potential to make a lasting impact. I dreamed of national recognition for our work, expansion into nearby cities, and securing multi-million-dollar grants. But reality quickly tempered my ambitions—I had a staff of just two, an office that trembled each time a train passed by, and I was stepping into a role that had been vacant for over eight months. My lofty dreams met a sobering reality check. I didn't know exactly where to start, but I knew I couldn't do it alone—I would need to lean on those around me.

As a nonprofit leader, you are constantly being pulled in different directions. You serve a mission greater than yourself, and many people are invested in your success. If you're leading a smaller organization, your job description likely includes tasks from multiple roles rolled into one. You may find yourself acting as Development Director, Head Custodian, and Event Planner all at once. In the midst of this juggling act, the best place to start is by understanding your ecosystem.

You've probably heard the term *ecosystem* in a scientific context, referring to the interconnected relationships between living organisms. In the nonprofit world, an ecosystem refers to the interconnected network of organizations, people, technology, platforms, and content that work together to fulfill your mission.

Who's in Your Ecosystem?

Do you know who makes up your ecosystem? Do you understand why they're connected to your organization? What other organizations in your community serve as partners or potential collaborators? Look closely at the people and entities directly tied to your mission—both internally and externally. These are the components of your ecosystem, and together, they keep your mission alive for those you serve.

A deep understanding of your ecosystem—who's in it and how they interact—forms the foundation of effective leadership. On that first day in my office, I realized that I needed to understand the people and groups already in place before I could jump into vision-setting or strategic planning. Successful leaders aren't those who come in with all the answers—they are the ones who ask the right questions and genuinely listen to the responses.

While each organization's ecosystem is unique, five key groups typically play an important role in fulfilling your mission:

1. Staff
2. Board of Directors
3. Donors

4. Volunteers
5. Community Partners

The size and role of these groups may vary depending on the scale of your organization. In a larger organization, you may have a sizable staff and dedicated volunteers who assist with service delivery. Conversely, in a smaller organization, you may rely heavily on volunteers to manage day-to-day tasks until you can afford to hire full-time staff. Regardless of size, you must ask the right questions to understand each group's motivations, challenges, and perspectives. Doing so will help you keep them engaged while identifying areas for improvement and growth.

Staff

Your staff is the engine that powers your organization's daily operations and mission fulfillment. They bring expertise, commitment, and time to your cause. Understanding their motivations, challenges, and ideas is crucial, as they have direct insight into what's working—and what's not—on the ground level. Their firsthand experience with clients or beneficiaries makes them invaluable for program development and organizational improvement.

Consider asking your staff these questions:

▸ What aspects of your role are working well, and where do you feel stuck or unsupported?
▸ How can leadership better support your personal and professional growth within the organization?

▸ Are there any processes or tools you believe could be improved to make your work more efficient?

▸ What's one thing about our organizational culture that you would like to see strengthened or changed?

▸ How do you see your work contributing to the mission of the organization?

Board of Directors

Your board provides strategic oversight, ensures fiduciary responsibility, and connects your organization to broader networks and resources. Board members bring diverse professional expertise and should be actively engaged in governance and long-term planning. You can maximize their strategic value to the organization by understanding their backgrounds and networks.

Consider asking your board the following questions:

▸ How do you perceive your role in advancing the organization's mission, and what support do you need to fulfill it?

▸ Are there specific areas of the organization's strategy or operations where you believe we need more focus or improvement?

▸ What do you see as the biggest challenges facing the organization in the next 1–3 years?

▸ How can we better leverage your expertise and connections to benefit the organization?

▸ What do you view as our greatest opportunities for growth or innovation?

Donors

Donors provide the financial foundation that sustains your mission. But beyond their financial contributions, they are investors in your cause who need to see the tangible impact of their support. Donors can also serve as thought partners, offering valuable insights as you develop and expand your programs and services. The more you engage with your donors, the stronger those relationships will become—helping you align funding opportunities with donor interests while maintaining program integrity.

Questions to ask donors:

▸ What inspired you to support our organization, and what keeps you engaged?
▸ Are there specific programs or initiatives you feel most connected to or passionate about?
▸ How do you prefer to receive updates on the impact of your contributions?
▸ Is there anything we can do differently to improve your donor experience?
▸ What motivates you to continue giving, and how can we better align with those motivations?

Volunteers

Volunteers multiply your organization's capacity and provide vital connections to the community. Volunteers bring fresh energy and perspective to your work whether they serve occasionally or regularly. Scheduling regular check-ins helps maintain engagement, improve the volunteer experience, and identify potential leadership volunteers who may eventually take on greater responsibilities—or even transition to staff roles.

Questions to ask volunteers:

▸ What led you to volunteer with us, and what keeps you coming back?

▸ How do you feel about the training and resources provided to support your volunteer efforts?

▸ What has been the most rewarding part of volunteering with us, and what could make it even better?

▸ Are there any barriers or challenges you face when contributing your time or skills?

▸ How do you see your volunteer work making an impact, and what additional feedback or support would you like?

Community Partners

I have always believed in the profound ability of nonprofits to drive significant change in the world. However, even with a great mission, partnerships amplify impact. You don't have to do this work alone—and you shouldn't! Strategic partnerships with other organizations and community stakeholders strengthen your reach and prevent duplication of services. These partnerships can range from informal collaborations to formal service agreements. They create opportunities for joint programming, resource sharing, and collective impact initiatives. By understanding your partners' priorities, constraints, and capabilities, you can build mutually beneficial relationships that better serve your shared community.

Questions to ask community partners:

▸ How do you view the relationship between our organization and yours? What's working well?

▸ Are there any unmet needs in the community that you believe we could help address?

▸ How can we collaborate more effectively to achieve shared goals?

▸ What do you see as the most pressing challenges in the community, and how can we better align our efforts to address them?

▸ Is there anything we could do to improve communication or coordination between our organizations?

The conversations you've had with those in your ecosystem are only valuable if they lead to action. Your next steps should involve taking what you've learned, identifying gaps, pulling out recurring themes, and using this information to inform future decisions.

Take time to systematically review all the feedback you've gathered. Look for common themes and concerns across different groups. For example, if both board members and staff mention challenges with internal communication, this should be flagged as a priority. To stay organized, create a simple document that categorizes feedback into three buckets:

1. **Immediate needs**: Issues that require urgent attention.

2. **Long-term considerations**: Goals that require sustained focus and planning.
3. **Resource-dependent improvements**: Enhancements that may require additional funding, staffing, or tools.

Prioritize and Plan

Once you've categorized the feedback, the next step is prioritization. Remember—you're only one person, and not everything can (or should) be addressed at once. Review your list and focus on:

▸ **Quick wins** that build momentum and demonstrate responsiveness.
▸ **Critical issues** that affect multiple groups or key functions of your organization.
▸ **Opportunities** that align with your current strategic priorities.
▸ **Emerging issues** that could escalate into larger problems if left unaddressed.

After identifying your priorities, create a basic action plan with clear timelines. This doesn't need to be overly complex—a simple spreadsheet that tracks what needs to be done, by whom, and by when will suffice. For example, you might include an action item to review and improve communication processes between staff and board members, with a goal of completing this within two weeks. The key is to set realistic timelines and ensure that feedback is transformed into actionable steps.

Communicate and Follow Up

Effective communication is crucial during this process. Once you've developed your action plan, circle back to those who provided input. Let them know what you heard, what you plan to do, and what may need to wait. People generally understand constraints if you're transparent about them. Sharing even a high-level version of your action plan shows that their feedback is being taken seriously and turned into tangible change.

As you begin implementing changes, pay close attention to their impact. Are the changes delivering the desired results? Have they led to any unintended consequences? Be ready to adjust your approach based on what you learn. This might involve modifying timelines, revising tactics, or even reconsidering certain solutions altogether.

Make Feedback an Ongoing Practice

Understanding your ecosystem is not a one-time event—it's an ongoing process. The conversations you're having today will evolve as your organization grows and as new challenges and opportunities arise. One of the best practices you can adopt is to create regular opportunities for feedback. This not only helps you catch potential issues early but also demonstrates your commitment to continuous improvement. Maintaining open channels of communication keeps everyone in your ecosystem engaged, as they see their input actively shaping the organization's direction.

Remember: Keep your door open, your ears alert, and your ego in check. The answers you're seeking are often already in the room—you just need to create the space for them to emerge.

CHAPTER 2

Know Your Data

" *Data is not just numbers—it's a story waiting to be told, and the better you listen, the stronger your decisions will be."*

Before I entered the nonprofit sector, I was a classroom teacher. While my title may have changed, many of the skills I honed in the classroom carried over and greatly informed my approach as a nonprofit leader. One of the most valuable practices I brought with me was the use of data. Anyone who's ever taught knows how integral data is to the instructional process, from start to finish. Data results in decisions about curriculum, pacing, student support, and more. On a broader level, data determines whether a school is considered successful and influences critical decisions about academic programs.

As a teacher, knowing my numbers was essential. I vividly recall afternoons spent at my desk, reviewing assessment data after giving quarterly or semester exams. After entering grades into my grade book, I would analyze the results—identifying which students performed well and which ones struggled. This data directly informed my next instructional steps.

Sometimes, exam results indicated the need to slow down and revisit a concept, meaning we would spend an additional week or two reviewing and practicing. Other times, the data showed that students had mastered the material and were ready to move on—perhaps even at a faster pace than I had initially planned. In both scenarios, I used data to guide my decisions, ensuring I wasn't relying solely on my assumptions or personal preferences. Instead, my choices were informed by actual results. The data influenced my pacing, the types of assignments I created, and how frequently I assessed students, both formally and informally.

Of course, data never told the whole story. I always followed up with students to gain additional context, but it provided a solid starting point and kept me on the right track. Without that data, I risked making decisions that, despite my best intentions, might not have served my students' long-term success. This same data-focused mindset became invaluable when I transitioned into nonprofit leadership.

Know Your Numbers

In your role as a nonprofit leader, chances are you have frequent interactions with donors—whether informally at networking events, in passing while running errands or during formal one-on-one meetings over lunch. Over the years, I've had hundreds of donor conversations, and while each is unique, many share common themes. In most of these conversations, donors ask questions about our program's performance, our impact, and our financial sustainability.

Here are some typical questions you might hear from donors:

- ▸ How many individuals did you help last month, quarter, or year?
- ▸ What is your impact goal for the upcoming year?
- ▸ How many people do you hope to add to your program in the next year?
- ▸ If I donate X dollars, how many more people could you serve?

Just as I had to be familiar with my students' performance data in the classroom, I now have to be equally familiar with my organization's data. Simply put, knowing your numbers is a fundamental part of any leadership role—and it's likely a critical part of yours, too.

In the same way data informed my instructional decisions as a teacher, it now informs my decisions as a nonprofit leader. It helps me articulate our impact to donors, set realistic goals, and identify areas where we need to improve or expand. Without this data, I wouldn't be able to answer critical questions or demonstrate the value of our work to stakeholders. And when you're responsible for leading an organization, securing funding, and maintaining trust with your community, knowing your numbers isn't just helpful—it's essential.

Informed Leadership Starts with Knowing Your Data

In my first few days on the job, I made what I like to call a "nonprofit no-no." I met with a longtime donor without doing my homework beforehand. I arrived at the coffee meeting energized and excited, armed with brochures and ready to share my vision as the new Executive Director. I had my goals in mind and was prepared to talk about them.

Early in the conversation, however, the donor asked, *"Can you tell me a little bit about what you know about me and my giving history with your organization?"* I froze. Unfortunately, I stumbled through an incorrect answer regarding their history with our nonprofit. It was a humbling moment—a clear example of not knowing my numbers. I hadn't done the necessary preparation, and it showed.

Whether it's your program's impact data, financial metrics, or a donor's giving history, it's necessary to stay informed. Knowing your numbers ensures that you're equipped to make sound decisions and engage meaningfully with stakeholders.

You Don't Need to Memorize Everything

Let me add a quick caveat: you don't need to memorize every piece of data about your organization. I'm not suggesting you spend the next few days trying to absorb every detail from your organization's database. However, you should have key numbers on your mind when going into meetings and conversations. For deeper, more complex metrics—such as financial history or program performance—prepare in advance, especially if you know you'll be speaking with a potential funder or key stakeholder.

Being prepared with relevant data shows that you are aware of your organization's current state and committed to its success. It also ensures you're ready to seize potential opportunities when they arise.

Being Data-Informed, Not Just Data-Driven

Just as I used data in the classroom to shape my teaching decisions, data is equally critical in nonprofit leadership. That's why being a data-informed leader is vital. *Being data-informed* means using data as a tool to guide decisions while balancing it with context, experience, and human factors. This approach differs from being purely *data-driven*, where decisions rely solely on quantitative metrics without considering qualitative factors.

A data-informed leader understands that while numbers are significant, they don't always tell the whole story. This means balancing measurable metrics with insights from lived experiences, feedback, and observations.

For example, if attendance at your youth program drops, a purely data-driven approach might suggest cutting the program. However, a data-informed leader would look beyond the numbers—gathering feedback from participants, considering external factors affecting attendance, evaluating long-term impact potential, and assessing community needs. This holistic approach leads to better, more thoughtful decisions that serve the organization's mission and stakeholders.

Types of Data You Need to Know

In your role, data is everywhere—from the frequency of virtual meetings to patterns of donor giving. Here are the three key categories of data you should be familiar with:

1. Operational Data

Operational data reflects how your organization functions on a day-to-day basis. This includes metrics such as program attendance, service delivery numbers, and staff or volunteer hours. Operational data provides insight into how well your organization is performing and highlights areas that may need improvement.

This data is fundamental for making budgeting decisions, identifying resource needs, and determining which funding sources to pursue. Staying on top of operational data helps ensure that your organization remains efficient and well-resourced.

> **Tip:** Create a simple weekly scorecard to track key metrics. This could include program participation rates, hours logged by staff and volunteers, or the number of services delivered. Review the scorecard at the start of each week to clearly understand what's happening on the ground. Doing this regularly helps you make data-informed decisions and address issues proactively.

Additionally, involve your staff in reviewing operational data. Hold monthly team meetings where staff can share their insights and observations. This approach combines quantitative data with real-world experience, giving you a more comprehensive understanding of your organization's operations.

2. Impact Data

Impact data shows how your programs are creating change in the community. It goes beyond counting numbers—it tells the story of your mission. From individual success stories to broader community improvements, impact data demonstrates the tangible results of your work.

Impact data is crucial for communicating your value to stakeholders, including funders, donors, and community partners. It shows not only what you do but how you're making a difference.

To effectively manage impact data, establish a consistent collection and analysis process. For example, schedule quarterly deep-dive sessions where you review program outcomes, participant progress, and community-level changes. Use these sessions to reflect on what's working, identify areas for improvement, and celebrate successes.

> **Tip:** Turn your findings into accessible reports that combine statistics with stories. These reports can be shared with stakeholders to highlight your organization's achievements and reinforce the value of their support.

It's important to remember that impact data often takes time to fully materialize. Establish both short-term and long-term measurement frameworks to capture meaningful outcomes. Avoid making hasty decisions based on early data alone—give yourself enough time to see the complete picture of your impact.

3. Financial Data

The third type of data is financial data, which reflects how well your organization manages and utilizes its monetary resources. This data tracks everything from program costs to fundraising success. As you may recall, financial data was exactly what I failed to review before my meeting with that longtime donor. Beyond just showing your organization's bank balance, financial data provides insight into how effectively you manage donor relationships, allocate resources, and plan for long-term sustainability. Regularly monitoring financial data enables you to make better decisions about your organization's future while ensuring you have the necessary funding to continue your mission.

Financial data requires consistent, structured review. Monthly financial review sessions should go beyond a simple examination of profit and loss statements. Key indicators to monitor include:

- ▸ Cost per program participant
- ▸ Fundraising return on investment (ROI)
- ▸ Cash flow projections

As a leader, you should establish clear financial benchmarks and regularly monitor trends that might affect your organization's sustainability. These insights will help you make proactive decisions about resource allocation, fundraising strategies, and program investments. Additionally, sharing relevant financial data with your board and leadership team ensures that everyone has a clear understanding of both the organization's opportunities and its limitations. (In the next chapter, I'll delve deeper into financial literacy and how to approach nonprofit finances.)

Data as a Leadership Tool

Reflect on your recent meetings with various stakeholders across your ecosystem. Which type of data—operational, impact, or financial—would have been most helpful during those conversations? Familiarity with your data doesn't just make you a better leader; it empowers your stakeholders to engage more effectively with your organization's mission. Your next funding opportunity might hinge on a data-informed conversation.

When you know your numbers, you're better equipped to:

▸ Tell your story with confidence
▸ Respond to challenges proactively
▸ Seize new opportunities as they arise

This familiarity allows you to have meaningful conversations with donors about program expansion, demonstrate to your board how their strategic decisions impact daily operations, and show community partners why collaboration is vital.

Remember: Data doesn't have to be your enemy, and metrics don't have to feel overwhelming. Instead, view data as a tool to help you lead with clarity, make informed decisions, and drive your organization's mission forward.

CHAPTER 3
Master Financial Literacy

Understanding your finances is not merely a skill—it's a superpower that shapes your future."

I stared at the budget spreadsheet on my screen, and the longer I stared, the more confused I became. It didn't take long to realize I had inherited a complex financial situation, and despite my years of program experience, I felt entirely out of my depth. I remember thinking, *"I'm great at serving our community—why is it so hard for me to get a grasp on these numbers?"* I tried to make sense of the budget categories, line items, and endless reports, but nothing seemed to click. Even with my education and program development background, understanding an entire organization's financial landscape was more challenging than I had anticipated.

I had multiple conversations with our treasurer, but each meeting left me with more questions than answers. My breaking point came during a crucial board meeting. A board member asked what seemed like a simple question about our cash flow projections, and I froze. The room suddenly felt hot as all eyes turned toward me, waiting for an explanation I barely understood myself. That moment made me realize that my discomfort with finances wasn't just affecting me—it undermined our organization's credibility and potentially jeopardized   future funding.

The following day, I made a pivotal decision: I would tackle our finances with the same dedication I had given to building our programs. I reached out to a fellow nonprofit executive who had mastered financial leadership and asked for advice. She reassured me: *"Everyone starts somewhere, and understanding your numbers is just another skill to learn—like grant writing or program development."*

For a long time, I believed that being a successful nonprofit leader was mostly about passion for the mission. While passion is undoubtedly important, I've since learned that great nonprofit leadership requires more—it requires building a solid financial foundation to support that mission.

The Reality of Nonprofit Leadership

Many nonprofit leaders come into their roles through program work, community organizing, or direct service. We may be experts in our mission areas, yet we often find ourselves navigating financial responsibilities without much guidance. However, understanding your organization's financial health is just as critical as understanding its programs.

You've probably heard the term *financial literacy* in the context of personal finance. I used to associate it with tracking expenses, managing a budget, and ensuring that you weren't spending more than you earned. In nonprofit leadership, financial literacy encompasses similar principles but on a larger scale. A financially literate leader understands how to:

▸ Interpret financial statements
▸ Manage cash flow effectively
▸ Make strategic financial decisions
▸ Guide the organization toward long-term financial health

Organizational financial literacy also includes budgeting, saving, and, in some cases, investing. Ultimately, the goal is to make financial decisions that strengthen the organization's overall sustainability.

Why Financial Literacy Matters

In the previous chapter, I highlighted financial data as one of the key types of data nonprofit leaders need to understand. Financial literacy goes hand in hand with this because it empowers you to make informed decisions, anticipate challenges, and engage confidently with stakeholders.

In many of my donor conversations—especially those that resulted in significant gifts—the turning point often came when donors asked, *"How much money will you need to hit this goal?"* If I didn't have a clear grasp of our cash flow or budget requirements, I couldn't answer with confidence. My ability to secure funding frequently depended on my understanding of our organization's financial picture.

If you're reading this and thinking, *"Is she saying I need to be a mathematician or an accountant to be a successful leader?"*—rest assured, I'm not. Many nonprofits either have a dedicated accountant or chief financial officer (CFO) on staff or outsource bookkeeping and financial reporting to an external accountant. While I strongly advocate for delegating these tasks to professionals with the right expertise, you still need to be able to:

▸ Interpret financial reports
▸ Explain key financial metrics to your board
▸ Communicate budget-related information to your team when necessary

Delegating financial management entirely without understanding it yourself can leave you in a vulnerable position. You don't want to be caught off guard when asked about your organization's finances or unable to provide clarity during important discussions.

Your Role in Financial Leadership

Even if you're not directly responsible for creating financial reports or entering data into accounting software, you need to understand key financial metrics such as:

▸ What's being spent
▸ Where funds are going
▸ How often expenses occur
▸ The impact of spending on your overall financial picture

If your board has a finance committee or a treasurer who leads the budgeting process, your role is to be an active participant. This means providing accurate information, offering context for financial decisions, and helping your board make well-informed choices. Financial leadership isn't about doing everything yourself—it's about ensuring you have enough knowledge to lead effectively, communicate clearly, and collaborate with financial experts to maintain the organization's financial health.

Own Your Numbers

First and foremost, it's essential to own your numbers. Even if you aren't the person creating financial reports, you are responsible for understanding them. Learn to read and interpret key financial statements like the balance sheet, income statement, and cash flow statement. If certain team members are responsible for individual budgets related to programs or events, take time to understand those budgets to keep expenses aligned with organizational goals. These financial documents tell the story of your organization's financial health, and clearly explaining that story to your board, team, and funders is a critical part of leadership.

Regularly Review Financial Reports

Develop a regular practice of reviewing financial reports. Set aside time each month to go over your organization's finances—block it on your calendar and give it your undivided attention. Pay close attention to trends, such as where you're spending the most and whether revenue is meeting projections. If something looks off compared to your expectations, make a note of it. Regularly reviewing financial reports helps you catch potential issues early, enabling you to make informed decisions and answer questions with confidence.

For example, if a program is running over budget on supplies, it's better to catch that issue one month into the program than six months later when adjustments are harder to make. Consistently reviewing financial data keeps your organization agile, responsive, and proactive.

Create a Financial Dashboard

Consider creating a **financial dashboard** that tracks the key metrics most relevant to your organization. This could include indicators like fundraising progress, grant spending, and operating reserves. A dashboard simplifies complex data into a format that's easy to monitor and share, making it easier to communicate financial performance to your board and funders.

Here's an example of what your dashboard might include:

- **Total Revenue YTD**: $XX,XXX
- **Total Expenses YTD**: $XX,XXX
- **Net Income/Deficit**: $XX,XXX (positive/negative)
- **Cash on Hand**: $XX,XXX (equivalent to X months of operations)
- **Individual Contributions**: $XX,XXX (X% of total revenue)
- **Grants**: $XX,XXX (X% of total revenue)
- **Event Revenue**: $XX,XXX (X% of total revenue)
- **Corporate Sponsorships**: $XX,XXX (X% of total revenue)

▶ **Program Costs**: $XX,XXX (X% of total expenses)

▶ **Salaries & Benefits**: $XX,XXX (X% of total expenses)

▶ **Fundraising Expenses**: $XX,XXX (X% of total expenses)

▶ **Administrative Costs**: $XX,XXX (X% of total expenses)

▶ **Fundraising Goal Progress**: $XX,XXX raised of $XX,XXX goal (X% complete)

(YTD – Year-to-date)

By building confidence in discussing financial matters, you demonstrate strong leadership and ensure that everyone—board members, staff, and funders—remains aligned with your organization's goals.

Connect Money to the Mission

Are you connecting money to your mission? This starts with understanding the true cost of delivering your programs. Don't just focus on direct expenses—consider indirect costs like administrative support, technology, and facilities.

I once attended a networking event where a donor, having read about our recent service area expansion, asked if I knew how much the expansion would cost. Because I was familiar with the numbers, I was able to give an immediate, accurate answer—and that response led to an on-the-spot donation. Knowing your numbers allows you to advocate effectively for financial support and ensures that your programs remain sustainable.

Your organization's budget should reflect your strategic priorities. Just as you can infer someone's personal priorities from their monthly spending, your organization's financial plan reveals what it values most. Every financial decision should be evaluated through the lens of mission impact: *How does each dollar spent move us closer to achieving our goals?*

This approach keeps your team focused on the big picture while maintaining financial accountability. It also provides clarity if budget cuts become necessary, as you can prioritize spending in alignment with strategic goals.

Diversify Your Revenue Streams

You might notice that most of your organization's funding comes from two or three key sources. While this isn't uncommon—especially for donor-funded programs—long-term financial stability depends on diversifying your revenue streams. Relying too heavily on a single source, like grants or donations, leaves your organization vulnerable.

For example, what happens to the program if a program is fully funded by a foundation grant that isn't renewed the following year? To avoid this risk, evaluate your current donor base and explore opportunities to diversify income through earned revenue, sponsorships, or major donor campaigns. Think about where you can expand your funding sources to ensure financial resilience.

Build Financial Partnerships

Building strong relationships with your finance team or accountant is crucial for effective leadership. If you outsource financial processes, maintain consistent communication with your external partners. Whether they're internal staff or external contractors, your finance team is a vital resource for interpreting data, identifying trends, and ensuring financial accuracy. Regular check-ins help you stay informed, ask questions, and manage budgets and reports collaboratively. Keeping these lines of communication open is especially important when anticipating changes or challenges.

Engage Your Board

Your board, particularly the finance committee (if you have one), plays a key role in ensuring the organization's financial health. Equip your board members with the tools and information they need to make informed decisions. This could mean pointing out declining donations or highlighting a significant new gift. Be transparent and proactive in sharing financial updates, even when things aren't going well. Open communication empowers your board to support problem-solving efforts, strengthening both your leadership and the organization's financial position. (In chapter six, I'll delve deeper into board member engagement.)

Involve Your Staff

Foster transparent communication to involve your staff in financial conversations. Use regular processes, such as monthly reports or dashboards, to keep everyone informed. If certain staff members manage their own budgets, ensure they have the knowledge and tools to do so effectively. Transparency builds trust, fosters collaboration, and aligns the team around your financial goals. When everyone understands the numbers, they're better equipped to support the mission.

Remember: Being financially literate as a leader doesn't mean becoming an accountant overnight. It means understanding enough to make informed decisions, communicate effectively, and lead with confidence.

PART 2

Relationships and Resources

" *Impact grows through meaningful connections and shared resources. When we align with others, we amplify the mission and extend our reach.*"

Visit www.myleadershipbook.com to download the Donor and Partner Mapping Activity

CHAPTER 4

Cultivate Donors Intentionally

Every donor is more than a transaction; they are a partner in your mission's success."

I still remember my first meeting with a major donor. It felt a lot like my first day of high school—filled with nervous anticipation. I put a lot of thought into how I would present myself that day, from what I wore to what I ate for breakfast. I wanted to go into this meeting as confident as possible. Unlike my previous mistake of showing up unprepared for a donor meeting, I had done my homework this time. I reviewed the donor's giving history in our database and made sure I was familiar with their past support.

I arrived at the coffee shop 15 minutes early, nervous enough that my leg shook uncontrollably, and I worried that the people at the next table might notice. This donor had invested significantly in our organization, and I didn't want to mess up. My goal was simple: show up as my best self, learn as much as I could about the donor, and cultivate a relationship that would encourage their continued support.

Early on in my career, I was told that fundraising should really be called *friendraising*. Building donor relationships reminded me of my middle school days, hoping a lunch table conversation would spark a new friendship. Unlike fleeting middle school friendships, I wanted this donor to feel deeply connected to our work and proud of the impact their donation had enabled.

During that meeting, I learned that the donor was passionate about our mission and enjoyed opportunities to see our work in action—whether through videos on social media or in-person site visits. As they shared their story, my nervousness turned into genuine excitement about keeping them engaged. We discussed my vision for the organization, plans for program expansion, and anticipated challenges. By the end of the meeting, not only had we scheduled a follow-up, but the donor also offered to introduce me to a potential board member.

Lessons in Donor Cultivation

That meeting was a turning point for me. It reinforced the importance of preparation and intentional relationship-building. Since that initial conversation, that donor has supported several of our programs and introduced us to others in their network. Over time, some of my most valuable strategic insights have come from donors who became trusted advisors—not just because they contributed financially, but because they also brought decades of experience, connections, and strategic thinking.

Keeping them engaged is crucial whether you're working with a donor who gives $100 or $100,000. It's always easier to cultivate existing donors than to prospect new ones, so prioritize nurturing those relationships. While donor cultivation can be a complex process, the lessons I learned in that first major donor meeting can be broken down into three simple steps:

1. Get to Know Them

As we discussed in the chapter on understanding your ecosystem, you need to truly get to know your donors. Yes, fundraising is important, but don't let financial goals overshadow the importance of building **authentic relationships**.

One-on-one conversations may not be feasible for every donor, but there are ways to connect with more donors at once. A couple suggestions include:

> ▸ **Host small donor events**: Use these gatherings to share updates and hear feedback from those who invest in your mission.
> ▸ **Send surveys**: Create online surveys to gather feedback on a recent program or initiative.

Of course, not every donor relationship will be smooth or energizing. Most nonprofit leaders can recount stories of difficult donors—those who test boundaries, make unreasonable demands, or try to micromanage how their gift is used. Some may push for special treatment, question practices without understanding the context, or require more time and attention than you can reasonably provide.

The key is to manage these relationships professionally while staying true to your organization's mission and values. Sometimes, this involves having tough conversations about boundaries or respectfully declining requests that don't serve your organization's best interests. In extreme cases, it may even mean gracefully declining future gifts from donors whose demands compromise your organization's integrity. Remember, while every donor deserves respect and appreciation, your primary responsibility is to your mission and the communities you serve.

2. Record What You Know

Over time, you'll meet with many donors—a sign that your organization is thriving. But as your donor base grows, it becomes harder to remember the specifics of each interaction. That's why it's crucial to record key details after every meeting. Whether it's an in-person coffee chat or a virtual conversation, capturing information promptly ensures nothing is forgotten.

My go-to strategy is to jot down key points right after a meeting, focusing on five key areas:

1. **Donor Motivation**: What excites the donor about your mission? Did they mention a specific program, story, or personal connection that resonates with them?
2. **Preferred Communication Style**: How do they prefer to stay in touch? Do they like email, phone calls, in-person meetings, or newsletters?

3. **Giving Capacity and Timing**: Did they indicate interest in giving or mention specific times when they are more likely to contribute? Are there key dates, like anniversaries or holidays, when they prefer to donate?

4. **Opportunities for Engagement**: Did they express interest in volunteering, attending events, or connecting with others who share their passion?

5. **Follow-Up Action Items**: Did they request specific follow-ups, such as additional information, reports, or an introduction to someone in your network?

For example, I might note that a donor prefers email over phone calls and always makes a donation in memory of a parent during a specific month. By recording this information, I can set a reminder to send a personalized note during that month, letting them know we're thinking of them.

Because I'm not always near my computer, I use a note-taking app on my phone to capture these details quickly, then transfer them to our donor software program later. If you don't have a donor management system, start with a simple spreadsheet to track key donor information, example below:

Donor First Name	Donor Last Name	Date of Meeting	Notes	Follow-Up Steps

The notes you take after donor meetings aren't just for your own memory—they help build a historical record for your organization. When I first started my role, I was fortunate that the previous Executive Director had kept detailed notes on all of our major donors. Thanks to those notes, I knew key details about each donor's preferred communication style, the best times of year to reach out, and the types of projects they were most interested in supporting.

Taking consistent notes allows you to be more prepared for future interactions and fosters stronger, more engaging relationships with donors. Remember: donors are people, too! While it's easy to focus solely on hitting fundraising goals, approaching donors as more than just financial contributors transforms how you engage with them and deepens the connection.

3. The Magic is in the Follow-Up

Congratulations—you've just had a productive meeting with a donor! Here's a hypothetical example of what they might have shared during your conversation:

▸ **They loved your recent newsletter**, especially the section about your new staff member and the projected 15% increase in services.

▸ **They first got involved with your organization** through a current board member who invited them to an event two years ago.

▸ **They're going on vacation for the next two months** and would like to be reminded to reconnect when they return.

Now that you've recorded these notes in your donor system or spreadsheet, it's time for the next step: **follow-up**. Cultivating donor relationships doesn't end with a great meeting— what you do afterward matters just as much. Here's how you could approach follow-up for the example above:

1. **Within 24 hours**: Send a personalized thank-you email. Specifically reference the donor's positive feedback about your newsletter and enthusiasm for your new staff member's potential impact. Acknowledge their ongoing support since attending that first event two years ago and confirm that you'll reach out after their vacation, as requested.

2. **Within 48 hours**: Complete your internal follow-up by updating their donor record. Note their connection to the board member who introduced them and their interest in your organization's growth and staff expansion. Set a reminder to follow up in two months when they return from vacation.

3. **At the two-month mark**: Send a thoughtful welcome-back email. Include relevant updates about your new staff member's impact, share metrics on your progress toward the 15% service increase, and subtly remind them of their connection to the board member. Consider inviting them to an upcoming event or a site visit to see your expanded services in action.

4. **Strengthen the relationship triangle**: Share appropriate highlights from the donor meeting

with the board member who made the introduction. Explore opportunities to deepen this interconnected relationship by involving the board member in future donor engagement efforts. Stronger connections between donors, board members, and your organization can lead to more sustained support over time.

Donor Relationships Are the Foundation of Fundraising

Building and maintaining strong donor relationships is integral to the success of any nonprofit organization. How you keep donors informed, engaged, and connected to your mission will directly influence your fundraising success.

This chapter didn't dive into detailed fund development plans or specific fundraising strategies because I believe that effective fundraising starts with relationship-building. Think about it—would you want someone asking you for money without first taking the time to get to know you? Probably not. When you invest time and effort upfront in cultivating genuine relationships, you'll see that effort pay off as you work toward your fundraising goals.

Over time, some of your donors may become trusted strategic advisors in your leadership journey. To make the most of these relationships:

▸ **Do your homework**: Know their giving history and interests.

▸ **Get to know them personally**: Understand what excites them about your mission.

▸ **Take detailed notes**: Capture key insights after every interaction.

▸ **Follow up consistently**: Keep the conversation going and show that you value their support.

Remember: By following this process, you'll build a strong foundation for garnering financial support—and perhaps even uncover wisdom and guidance from donors that prove more valuable than their financial contributions alone.

CHAPTER 5
Leverage Community Partnerships

❝ *Collaboration turns individual efforts into collective impact, creating ripples far beyond what one can do alone.*"

The more conversations I had with donors, the more my ideas began to expand. Each discussion unlocked new possibilities: potential program expansions, resources for staff, or tools to support the board. Many of these donors became strategic advisors, offering their expertise when challenges arose and serving as thought partners when I needed someone to debrief with. One donor, in particular, transformed my approach to problem-solving during one of our quarterly coffee chats. During these chats, they encouraged me to be open about my current challenges. On one occasion, I shared my frustration about an event we were trying to plan but couldn't proceed with due to venue issues.

Our organization wanted to host a celebration for our educators and use the event to introduce prospective donors to our mission. However, due to budget constraints, we couldn't find a suitable venue with the audiovisual capabilities we required and enough capacity for our attendees. Every venue we considered charged double our allocated budget. I had already started discussions with my team and board about restructuring the event to fit a more affordable location.

When I expressed my frustrations to the donor, they asked if I had considered partnering with a local venue that had recently come under new ownership. They explained that the new owner was eager to build the venue's brand and reach a new audience. They also noted that the owner had a history of supporting education-based organizations, which aligned well with our mission. Following this conversation, I immediately researched the venue, found a contact number, and left a message for the owner. To my surprise, the owner called back the next day. I mentioned the donor's referral, explained our organization's focus on supporting educators, and described our urgent need for a venue that could meet our technical and capacity requirements. I also clarified that the event aimed to celebrate the success of the educators we support and cultivate new donors for the coming year.

Before I could finish explaining our needs, the owner enthusiastically offered to host the event at no cost for the venue, provided we used their on-site catering services for beverages and refreshments. This partnership saved us thousands of dollars in event expenses.

Additionally, we formed a unique collaboration with the business, which was eager to increase its visibility and marketing reach. We included their logo on all event promotional materials and donor invitations. Although we had hosted fundraising events in the past, I had never considered partnering with a local business for a smaller, more informal gathering like this.

Initially, I didn't think to reach out to a local business for collaboration—I spent too much time trying to solve the problem on my own. This experience taught me the value of sharing challenges with others. When you voice your concerns, you open the door to collaboration and innovative solutions. I also learned the power of mutually beneficial partnerships, where both parties can succeed. Nonprofits often take on expansive missions, whether it's ending homelessness, supporting victims of abuse, or helping students improve academically through after-school programs. These goals are rarely achievable by a single organization alone. Real impact requires collaboration among multiple organizations and businesses.

This is why I believe that a core component of nonprofit leadership is understanding that the weight of the mission doesn't rest solely on one person or organization. Partnerships are essential to progress. In earlier chapters, I emphasized the importance of a strong board and a clear understanding of your ecosystem. However, I felt it was important to dedicate a chapter to building partnerships with other organizations and businesses.

You cannot fulfill your organization's mission alone. It takes a collective effort. I encourage you to think creatively about potential partnerships. Are you missing opportunities by not offering collaboration options?

Are there local businesses or organizations that could benefit from supporting your work while also achieving their goals? Exploring these possibilities can make a significant difference in achieving your mission. Furthermore, don't limit yourself to your immediate community—there may be organizations in other states or at the national level that share an aligned mission and would be eager to partner with you. Stay open-minded when it comes to building partnerships.

Once you've identified a potential partner, developing a mutually beneficial relationship is next. The following strategies can help you create a partnership that works for both parties:

Mission-Aligned Partners

When seeking community partnerships, the first step is to identify organizations that complement your work and align with your mission. These partners should share similar values and goals while focusing on areas that enhance, rather than duplicate, your efforts. For example, if your nonprofit is dedicated to improving literacy rates among children, a mission-aligned partner could be a local library or a youth mentorship organization. This approach fosters collaboration and prevents competition for resources, allowing both organizations to work together effectively toward a shared goal.

One key advantage of mission-aligned partnerships is the ability to create a symbiotic relationship, where each organization contributes unique strengths to fill gaps the other cannot address alone. You can amplify your collective impact by combining resources, expertise, and networks. For instance, if your organization provides after-school tutoring, partnering with another group offering free meals or mental health services can create a more comprehensive support system for your audience. You gain access to additional resources while your partner expands their reach to a new group.

To find mission-aligned partners, start by conducting a community scan to identify organizations operating in related fields. Research their goals, programs, and impact to determine if their work complements yours. Reach out to their leadership teams to discuss potential collaboration opportunities. Successful partnerships are built on a shared vision and trust, so take the time to establish genuine connections. These initial conversations can reveal creative ways to combine efforts for mutual benefit. During these discussions, clearly define roles and expectations to ensure a productive partnership. Effective collaboration requires a clear understanding of each partner's contributions and what success looks like. Mission alignment goes beyond shared values—it's about building partnerships that allow both organizations to thrive while delivering meaningful outcomes for the communities you serve.

Develop a Joint Project

Starting small with shared initiatives is a great way to test a partnership and build trust over time. Collaborative projects allow organizations to work together toward a common goal, creating opportunities to learn about each other's strengths, communication styles, and areas for growth. A successful joint project can lay the groundwork for deeper collaboration while demonstrating to stakeholders the tangible value of working in partnership. These initiatives don't need to be complex or costly—they can be as simple as co-hosting an event, running a social media campaign, or sharing resources to serve a common audience.

One of my favorite events was one I planned in collaboration with two other nonprofits. Both organizations worked directly with children in different neighborhoods, and together, we hosted a joint event for all our donors. The goal was to increase brand awareness and spread the word about our ongoing work. However, we weren't entirely sure of the best approach to achieve that. We knew we wanted a venue that encouraged networking among attendees while providing an opportunity for them to engage with program participants. The event was designed to introduce our work and highlight the power of partnership in strengthening the community.

Over three months, we held regular planning meetings to develop a budget, set intended outcomes, and assign responsibilities. Each organization brought its unique expertise to the table: one focused on community outreach, another handled logistics and coordination, while my team created promotional materials and managed donor invitations. We deliberately kept the event manageable by concentrating on shared goals rather than attempting to showcase every aspect of our work. This streamlined approach kept us aligned and prevented us from feeling overwhelmed.

The event exceeded our expectations, meaningfully bringing together donors, volunteers, and program participants. Donors appreciated seeing the collaboration firsthand and understanding how their support extended beyond a single organization to create a broader community impact. By starting small and working together on this initiative, we built trust and rapport among our teams, setting the stage for future collaborations.

Formalize Agreements

As partnerships grow, moving beyond informal arrangements and formalizing the relationship through clear documentation. Memorandums of Understanding (MOUs) are a valuable tool for defining roles, expectations, and desired outcomes. While they may seem overly formal for smaller collaborations, MOUs help establish a mutual understanding and serve as a guide to keep both organizations aligned. They also protect both parties by clearly outlining responsibilities, timelines, and any financial or resource contributions.

One key advantage of using an MOU is that it helps prevent misunderstandings. By explicitly defining who is responsible for specific tasks and how success will be measured, you reduce the risk of assumptions that can lead to conflict. For example, if one partner is responsible for marketing and the other for securing a venue, documenting these expectations ensures there's no overlap or missed responsibilities. An MOU also enhances accountability by providing a clear reference point if challenges arise during the partnership.

Drafting an MOU doesn't have to be complicated. Start by including:

- The purpose of the partnership
- A detailed list of responsibilities for each organization
- A timeline for the initiative
- Agreed-upon outcomes

Additionally, outline how decisions will be made and how potential conflicts will be resolved. While legal language can help ensure clarity, you should keep the document accessible to all parties. If the partnership involves significant financial commitments or long-term collaboration, consider having the MOU reviewed by legal counsel to ensure it adequately protects both organizations.

Even for smaller projects, formalizing agreements builds trust and professionalism. It shows a commitment to accountability and ensures that all parties are aligned from the outset. Whether the collaboration is a short-term initiative or the beginning of a long-term partnership, an MOU provides a solid foundation for success and sets the tone for how your organizations will work together toward shared goals.

Remember: Collaboration strengthens your ecosystem. Building partnerships rooted in mutual benefit strengthens your organization and positions you for collective impact. When you collaborate effectively, you expand your reach, pool resources, and amplify your mission's impact.

CHAPTER 6
Strengthen Board Engagement

A strong board isn't built overnight—it's cultivated through trust, shared vision, and accountability."

Working alongside a Board of Directors has been a continuous learning experience for me. When I first stepped into nonprofit leadership, I inherited a board of 15 members who had been involved for years. It was overwhelming. I had to figure out my role, adjust my leadership style, and—most importantly—build relationships with this group. They were responsible for governing the organization, evaluating my performance as the senior leader, and partnering with me to fulfill our mission.

I had no idea how to manage our working relationship at the time. During my first few board meetings, I didn't speak much. I came prepared with my laptop, ready to take notes, but mostly, I just listened. Even when I had ideas or feedback, I hesitated to share them. Part of my reluctance came from being new to the role, but I also wasn't sure how to balance the power dynamic with the board. I had experience in education and knew how schools operated. I even understood how local school boards functioned in partnership with super-intendents. Yet, transitioning to nonprofit leadership felt like an entirely different challenge.

By the time I started finding my footing, things became more complicated. Our board was technically composed of 15 members, but in reality, it didn't feel that way. Some members rarely showed up to meetings or responded to emails, leaving me unsure if they even wanted to remain on the board. Others attended meetings but barely contributed, saying only a few things here and there. Meanwhile, a small core group of about five members dominated discussions, led initiatives, and drove decision-making. This core group was engaged, committed, and willing to fundraise, which was great—but it meant we weren't operating at full capacity. It didn't take long for me to realize how much this imbalance could impact our long-term success.

The Board-ED Relationship: A Balancing Act

One of the most important lessons I've learned is that the relationship between an Executive Director (ED) and the board is a delicate balancing act. Sometimes, as the ED, you lead the board—guiding them through strategy and initiatives. Other times, such as during evaluations or salary discussions, the board leads you. This dynamic can feel like walking a tightrope, requiring trust, communication, and mutual respect.

If you've worked with a board, you know how critical it is to have an engaged and committed group. And if you haven't had that experience yet, trust me—it makes a world of difference. A strong board isn't just there to provide governance; they're your best ambassadors, advocates, and supporters, helping to spread the word and advance the mission.

The Board of Directors plays a vital role in oversight, guidance, and ensuring accountability. They support your organization's strategy, monitor effectiveness, and ensure that operations are both legal and ethical. With such significant responsibility, the pressure on the board can be immense. That's why the partnership between an organization's leadership and its board is essential.

If your organization were an airplane, think of the board and the ED as co-pilots. Both are accountable to one another, and both are essential for ensuring the plane reaches its destination safely. Building a strong board-leader relationship doesn't happen overnight. It requires intentional effort—navigating roles, finding common ground, and aligning around shared goals. When this partnership clicks, it provides steady hands-on control, helping the organization not only stay in the air but also soar to new heights.

Strategies for Strengthening Board Engagement

I want to see your organization soar, and that starts with building a strong partnership with your board. It won't happen instantly—it took me years to develop effective relationships with my board members. For me, it required some members to step away to pursue other opportunities that were better aligned with their goals and onboarding new members eager to contribute their skills. Once we collectively put in the work, we saw real results: a more aligned organization and a stronger partnership. You can achieve the same by setting a solid foundation for success using the following strategies:

Strategy 1: Set Clear Expectations

Many board issues stem from a lack of clarity around roles and responsibilities. As a leader, it's your responsibility to ensure that everyone understands what's expected of them. If you have an executive committee (usually composed of a chair, vice-chair, secretary, and treasurer), work with them to develop clear expectations for both onboarding new members and assessing the performance of current ones.

How to Set Expectations:

▸ **Develop Board Member Job Descriptions**: Create detailed role descriptions that outline time commitments, committee participation, and fundraising responsibilities. For example, clarify whether board members are expected to secure specific donation amounts or dedicate a set number of hours each month. Just as with an employment job description, this document should communicate qualifications for the role and highlight skills the board needs.

▸ **Host New Member Onboarding Sessions**: Provide new board members with a thorough orientation covering the organization's mission, strategic goals, and their role in achieving those goals. Think of it like onboarding a new employee—smooth transitions lead to better engagement. A well-structured onboarding session ensures new members understand the organization's context and their responsibilities from the start.

▸ **Create an Annual Calendar**: Outline key events, meetings, and fundraising deadlines so board members can proactively plan their involvement. Many leaders become frustrated when board members miss meetings or events, but often, this happens because dates aren't communicated in advance. Create an annual calendar at the start of each fiscal year and share it with your board. Remember: if it's not on their calendar, it likely won't happen.

When board members have clear expectations about their roles and responsibilities, it becomes easier to hold them accountable. You can't expect board members to be engaged and active if you haven't defined what those terms mean in the context of your organization. Clear expectations help leaders manage board engagement and enable board members to assess their performance annually, using these expectations as criteria. You can't evaluate what's unclear—these defined expectations give the board a framework to identify what's working well and where changes may be necessary.

Strategy 2: Engage Through Committees

Committees allow board members to focus on areas where they can have the most impact. They also prevent the full board from becoming overwhelmed with operational details. More importantly, committees help the board share in the organization's work   .

In some nonprofits, I've seen Executive Directors try to lead staff and do all the work of the board, which is unrealistic and unsustainable. Committees distribute responsibility, allowing board members to contribute meaningfully to the organization's overall operations.

While the specific committees you establish will depend on your organization's mission, common committee types include:

- ▸ **Executive Committee**: This smaller decision-making body typically consists of the board chair, vice-chair, secretary, and treasurer. The executive committee handles urgent matters between board meetings and provides leadership for the board as a whole.
- ▸ **Governance Committee**: This committee is responsible for maintaining the board's health and effectiveness. It handles recruiting, onboarding, and training new board members. It also oversees board evaluations and ensures compliance with bylaws and governance best practices.
- ▸ **Finance Committee**: This committee oversees the organization's financial planning and performance. It reviews and approves budgets,

monitors financial health, and ensures proper financial controls and audits are in place.

▶ **Programs Committee**: Depending on your non-profit's focus, this committee ensures that programs align with the mission and strategic goals. It monitors program effectiveness, provides input on planning and evaluation, and supports staff in identifying improvements. Smaller organizations often rely on this committee to assist directly with program development.

▶ **Fundraising Committee**: This committee is dedicated to securing the financial resources necessary to sustain the organization. It develops and executes fundraising strategies, identifies potential donors, and engages the entire board in fundraising efforts.

▶ **Ad Hoc Committees**: These are temporary committees formed to address specific needs or projects, such as developing a strategic plan. Once the task is completed, the committee disbands.

When assigning members to committees, consider their skills and interests. For instance, a board member with a background in finance might serve on the finance committee, while someone with marketing expertise could join the fundraising or programs committee. Each committee should have measurable goals to focus its efforts. For example, the fundraising committee might set a goal of increasing monthly giving by 20% by hosting quarterly donor prospecting events.

Every committee should have a designated chair responsible for leading meetings and reporting progress to the full board. This structure keeps everyone accountable and ensures that committees remain focused on achieving their objectives.

Strategy 3: Foster Strong Relationships

Strong board-leader partnerships are built on trust and mutual respect. Just as you invest time in building relationships with donors and staff, it's equally important to do so with your board. A collaborative and supportive board culture starts with intentional relationship-building.

If you're looking to strengthen your relationships with board members—or enhance the good ones you already have—I recommend starting with one-on-one meetings. When I became Executive Director, I prioritized these meetings during my first few weeks and continued them regularly, aiming to meet with each board member at least twice a year. Time passes quickly, and without a deliberate effort, it's surprisingly easy to go over a year without personally connecting with individual board members.

These meetings proved invaluable. For example, when a board member's attendance began to wane, a one-on-one conversation helped me understand their situation and offer support until they were ready to re-engage. These personal interactions allow you to understand their motivations, address concerns, and align their contributions with the organization's needs.

Recognition Matters

Who doesn't appreciate being recognized for their hard work? Board members volunteer their time because they believe in your mission and want to see your organization succeed. While they don't might not rewards, genuine recognition makes them feel valued and energized.

You don't need to spend a lot of money on fancy plaques or awards. Simple gestures, such as handwritten thank-you notes or public recognition in newsletters, go a long way. You might also consider hosting an annual board appreciation event at the end of the fiscal year to celebrate their efforts.

Encourage Open Communication

Creating a culture of open communication is key to a strong board-leader relationship. Board members should feel comfortable sharing ideas, asking questions, and providing feedback. As I mentioned earlier, the most effective organizations are those where the board and leadership maintain open, transparent communication.

As a leader, it's essential to foster an environment where ideas can flow freely in both directions. This kind of openness fosters innovation and   helps identify potential challenges early, allowing your organization to address them proactively.

Remember: When you prioritize open communication, align board members around a shared vision, and empower them with clear roles and responsibilities, you create a board that's not just supportive but actively engaged and invested in your mission. A well-engaged board helps your organization move forward with confidence and clarity.

PART 3

Leadership in Action

" *Leadership is more than strategy—it's about inspiring, empowering, and creating momentum that transforms visions into realities."*

Visit www.myleadershipbook.com to download the Leadership Reflection and Team Alignment Activity.

CHAPTER 7

Develop Your Team

" A thriving team is the heartbeat of a successful mission. Invest in them and watch your work blossom."

"You know, I can help you with that, right?"

I paused, looked over my shoulder, and saw my administrative assistant approaching as I stood at a table, stuffing over 300 envelopes for our upcoming newsletter mailing.

I smiled and replied, "Yeah, thanks, but I think I can handle it. I appreciate you asking," and went back to my self-imposed assembly line of stamps, envelopes, and newsletters. She waited a few seconds, laughed, and said, "No, really, I can take this off your hands. This is actually part of my job, you know."

This wasn't the first time we'd had this kind of exchange. Whether it was following up with a donor, mailing newsletters, or setting up refreshments for a board meeting, she often had to remind me that she was hired to do many of the tasks I insisted on handling myself.

That day, standing in front of hundreds of newsletters, I took a moment to reflect on what she'd said. After a brief pause, I finally responded, "You know what?

You're right. I'll let you handle this." I invited her over to my makeshift mailing station and walked her through my process of stuffing, stamping, sealing, and labelling the newsletters. Then, I did something that had been surprisingly difficult for me—I handed the task over and stepped away.

To my surprise, she completed the task quickly, freeing up my time to work on a crucial   grant application that was due in just a few days. When she finished, she popped her head into my office and asked if there was anything else she could help with. That opened the door for me to delegate a few more tasks that had been piling up on my plate.

As a recovering perfectionist and admittedly Type A, I realized something crucial: I needed to stop doing everything myself. Not only did I need to let my administrative assistant do the job she was hired for, but I also needed to trust her—and others on my team—to take ownership of tasks that they were capable of handling (and eager to help with).

Building a Delegation Culture

In the days that followed, I scheduled a one-on-one conversation with my administrative assistant to discuss her role more thoroughly. I apologized for overstepping and not giving her the opportunity to fully own her responsibilities. I also invited her to share any ideas about other tasks or projects she wanted to take on. She expressed an interest in supporting donor events, assisting with board meetings, and helping set up for in-person programs. Together, we made a plan to involve her more in these areas, and I created a system for delegating tasks while ensuring she felt supported as she learned new processes.

Over time, I've learned that delegating is not just okay—it's critical. My role as a leader isn't to do everything myself but to support, empower, and develop my team members so they can confidently lead and own their work. Rather than being a solo leader who tries to handle it all, I could rely on my team to help bring the organization's vision to life, even if we were a small group.

Overcoming Delegation Challenges

If you're someone who struggles with delegation, you're not alone. Maybe you worry that the quality of work won't meet your standards. Perhaps you're hesitant because you want things done "your way." Or perhaps you've always had to do everything yourself and find it hard to adjust to having others take over tasks you once handled solo.

When I think about sustainability in leadership and nonprofit organizations, developing and trusting your team ranks high on the list. You can't build a lasting, impactful organization if everything rests on your shoulders. Whether you lead a team of two or fifty, your goal should be to foster a culture where everyone takes ownership of their work and contributes to the organization's mission in meaningful ways.

Here's the reality: you'll burn out if you try to do everything alone. But when you invest in your team—leveraging their skills, empowering them to lead, and trusting them to take responsibility—you create a sustainable organization capable of long-term success.

Start with Small Releases

In your current role, what projects are on your plate that you could delegate to smaller sections? Delegation isn't about dumping a large project on someone's lap and calling it "empowering." True delegation—when done well—develops your team by providing clear explanations, answering questions, and offering support as needed.

The most effective development happens when you approach delegation as a teaching opportunity rather than just a task hand-off. Think about your own experience learning new skills—you likely had someone who took the time to explain not only *what* to do but also *why* it mattered and how it fits into the bigger picture. When you delegate with this mindset, you're not simply clearing your to-do list; you're investing in your team's growth and future capacity.

I can reflect on moments in my career when leaders told me they were "developing my leadership" but, in practice, simply handed me large projects without guidance or support. I felt unprepared and isolated—exactly the opposite of what actual development should feel like. What I needed in those moments were clear instructions, ongoing support when I ran into challenges, and perhaps a framework or template to help me get started.

When delegating, consider using this approach:

1. Identify Starter Tasks

Begin with small, manageable tasks that align with the team member's current skills and offer opportunities for growth. Examples include:

- ▸ Drafting emails
- ▸ Organizing meeting notes
- ▸ Conducting preliminary research

These tasks allow team members to build confidence while contributing meaningfully to the organization.

2. Provide Clear Instructions

When handing off a task, explain what needs to be done in clear, actionable terms. Share any relevant guidelines, templates, or examples to help clarify your expectations. Additionally, communicate how the task connects to the broader organizational goal, so the team member understands its significance.

3. Encourage Questions and Independence

Create an environment where team members feel comfortable asking questions, both before starting the task and as they work through it. Encouraging independence doesn't mean abandoning them; it means supporting them while allowing space for autonomy and problem-solving.

Gradual Delegation: Building Confidence Over Time

This approach aims to prepare your team members to take on increasingly significant responsibilities in a way that aligns with their personal goals and the organization's needs. Instead of delegating entire projects upfront, start small by assigning tasks you feel comfortable explaining and guiding as needed. This gradual transition—from "doing it all" to "leading it all"—builds both trust and competence.

For example, you could start by delegating tasks like scheduling meetings or formatting reports. Once the team member becomes proficient in those areas, you can gradually move on to larger responsibilities, such as managing donor relations or overseeing entire program areas.

Have open conversations with your team members—similar to the one I had with my administrative assistant—to learn more about their interests and goals for skill development. Then, consider how you can delegate tasks or create new opportunities that help nurture those interests and skills. When you take this intentional approach, you lighten your workload and cultivate a more capable and confident team.

Create Learning Loops

How are you creating opportunities for your team members to learn? I've always appreciated professional development—attending conferences, taking courses, or listening to podcasts. I'll devour books on any topic I want to explore further. These are all great ways to build capacity and expand skills. However, when I reflect on my past work experiences before becoming an Executive Director, I realize there were few opportunities where I was truly given space to learn on the job.

By *learning*, I don't mean being thrown into difficult tasks without support and then judged on how well I performed. I mean having intentional opportunities for training: receiving clear guidance, being assigned a mentor or guide, having a plan in place, and getting follow-up throughout the process. Too often, especially in my early career as an educator, I was placed in challenging roles without any real support. True learning requires intentionality.

Fostering On-the-Job Learning

Establish a feedback system when team members take on new responsibilities to create an effective learning environment. This turns growth into a two-way conversation rather than a one-way delegation. Meet regularly to discuss what went wrong and what went well, what insights they gained, and how they'd approach the task differently next time.

For example, if you're delegating communications for an upcoming donor event to a fundraising team member, here's how a structured process might look:

Sample Learning Loop for Delegating a Donor Event

1. Initial Setup Meeting

▸ Share previous event communication examples and templates.

▸ Walk through the timeline and key milestones.

▸ Clarify what success looks like.

▸ Identify potential challenges and available resources.

2. Weekly Check-In Structure

▸ **Start with:** "What's working well in the process?"

▸ **Discuss:** "Where are you feeling stuck?"

▸ **Explore:** "What resources would help you move forward?"

▸ **Plan:** "What are your next steps before our next check-in?"

3. Post-Event Reflection

▸ Review key metrics (e.g., email open rates, RSVP responses, attendance).

▸ Discuss unexpected challenges that arose.

▸ Identify process improvements for future events.

▸ Document learnings and update templates.

▸ Celebrate wins and innovative approaches.

This structured approach allows your team members to grow while ensuring important details aren't missed. Most importantly, it creates a safe environment where asking questions is encouraged, and mistakes are seen as learning opportunities rather than failures.

Build Trust Through Transparency

At the core of fostering a learning environment are trust and transparency. Without these, even the best development opportunities fall flat. In workplaces lacking trust and transparency, you can often sense hesitation in communication, a lack of collaboration, and an underlying uncertainty among team members. People hold back ideas, avoid taking risks, and may even disengage entirely out of fear of being judged or misunderstood.

Leaders must intentionally cultivate trust and transparency to create a culture where open dialogue, mutual respect, and shared goals can thrive—allowing every team member to reach their potential.

I've always believed that trust and transparency start at the top. Share your own leadership journey, including mistakes you've made along the way. Leaders make mistakes, too, but it's easy to feel the pressure to always appear competent and in control. When leaders are open about their own growth and learning process, it creates psychological safety, making it easier for team members to take risks and learn.

For example, you might share a story about a time when you tried to handle everything yourself, leading to burnout or missed opportunities. Explaining how that experience shaped your current leadership approach helps humanize you and opens the door for greater transparency. I understand that leaders can be hesitant to share mistakes, but I've found that it strengthens relationships and trust when people see us as humans who don't always have it together .

Transparency also involves how you encourage others to share their ideas and how you handle feedback. Ask yourself:

▶ Do you create opportunities for team members to express when something isn't working?
▶ Is there space for pushback on ideas you propose?
▶ Are you open to receiving feedback when you've made a mistake?

If you aren't willing to model openness, you can't expect your team to be open either.

Developing Your Team with Intention

Think about the intentional steps you can take to further develop and support your team. Consider what resources, opportunities, and feedback you can offer to help them grow in their skills, confidence, and contributions. Reflect on how you can align their individual goals with the broader vision of the organization, fostering a sense of shared purpose and ownership.

Remember: Sometimes, the best thing you can do as a leader is to step back and allow others to step up. This doesn't mean stepping away entirely—it means creating space for your team members to take initiative, make decisions, and showcase their leadership potential.

CHAPTER 8

Tell Your Story Strategically

" *Stories inspire action. Tell yours with purpose, and the right people will rally to your cause.*"

Imagine leading a 15-year-old community-based organization and constantly meeting people who tell you they've never heard of your organization.

That's exactly where I found myself in 2019. After a few years in my role, I felt more confident in my leadership. I had a solid grasp of managing my team of employees and contractors. My daily schedule finally allowed for a balance between internal support and external engagement with partners and supporters. I had even managed to carve out a daily 45-minute lunch break—something I only started doing after realizing my morning coffee wasn't enough to keep me fueled throughout the day.

Despite these successes, one major challenge remained: our organization's brand awareness.

Leading a grassroots nonprofit felt empowering from the start. We didn't have a single founder—instead, several community members had come together to solve a problem they saw in their neighborhood. They didn't wait for someone else to fix it. They met regularly, did their own research, developed a solution, and secured funding on their own. Even now, thinking about their initiative fills me with pride. Being part of a legacy built by determined individuals who wanted to improve their community felt meaningful.

So, you can imagine my surprise—after three years in my role—when I kept hearing people in our service area say they didn't know we existed. Initially, I brushed it off as an isolated comment. But as we continued attending community fairs, festivals, and events, handing out branded flyers and pens, the same comments kept coming.

This forced me to confront a harsh truth: there was a disconnect between the story we thought we were telling and how the community actually perceived us. Simply being a "community-founded organization" wasn't enough—we had to be intentional about communicating our mission in a way that resonated with people. Without that intentionality, we'd continue encountering the same surprised reactions and miss out on the deeper connections we needed to build.

Nonprofit storytelling is defined as sharing your mission, values, and impact through stories that inspire and connect with others. These stories can come from a variety of sources—board members who work alongside you, beneficiaries who directly benefit from your services, or volunteers who contribute their time and effort. However, for stories to be effective, they need to be shared in a compelling and consistent way.

When I reflected on the feedback we received about our lack of awareness in the community, it became clear that I wasn't doing enough to communicate our impact effectively. We had a strong mission, a clear vision, and solid values, but they weren't being conveyed in a way that connected with the people we served. I knew I had to refine our storytelling approach if I wanted the organization to be sustainable .

Common Storytelling Channels for Nonprofits

Storytelling can take many forms. Below are the most common channels nonprofits use to share their narratives:

- ▶ **Websites**: Often the first place people visit to learn about a nonprofit's mission and impact. A well-designed website serves as a hub for success stories, upcoming events, and opportunities to get involved.
- ▶ **Social Media**: Platforms like Facebook, Instagram, X (formerly Twitter), LinkedIn, and TikTok allow users to share real-time updates, photos, videos, and stories. Social media helps humanize your organization by showing the faces behind the work.
- ▶ **Email Campaigns and Newsletters**: Regular email updates nurture relationships with donors, volunteers, and community members. Use this channel to share impact stories, announce upcoming events, and highlight new initiatives.

▸ **Annual Reports and Impact Reports**: These structured documents provide an opportunity to showcase successes, demonstrate transparency with finances, and highlight measurable impact. Incorporating photos, data visualizations, and personal testimonials makes these reports more engaging.

▸ **Video Content**: Videos can capture emotions and stories in ways that written content can't. Whether it's a short social media clip or a mini-documentary, video storytelling helps create a stronger emotional connection with your audience.

▸ **Events and Presentations**: In-person events such as galas, fundraisers, open houses, and community forums offer opportunities to connect directly with supporters. Live testimonials, interactive displays, and personal interactions make your mission tangible.

▸ **Podcasts and Audio Stories**: Sharing interviews, behind-the-scenes insights, and personal narratives via audio makes your work more intimate and accessible. Podcasts are particularly effective for supporters who prefer to consume content on the go.

▸ **Printed Collateral (Brochures, Flyers, Posters)**: Having physical materials available at community events, local businesses, and partner organizations ensures people can quickly understand who you are and how they can get involved.

▸ **Personal Testimonials and Case Studies**: Highlighting real experiences from those you serve or those who volunteer with you provides a powerful way to demonstrate your impact. These stories can be repurposed across multiple channels, from blog posts to social media.

▸ **Blogs and Online Articles**: Whether hosted on your website or published on platforms like Medium or LinkedIn, blogs offer a way to explore your mission more deeply, share stories of triumph and challenge, and explain the "why" behind your work.

In my role, I had to take a step back and assess how other nonprofits were successfully getting their message out. I noticed that many had revamped their websites with updated impact stories and data charts, while others shared behind-the-scenes videos on social media, showcasing the real people behind their mission. This prompted me to reassess the communication channels we were using and decide which additional platforms we could leverage to increase awareness.

At the time, we relied heavily on our website, newsletter mailings, and in-person presentations at events. I realized that social media was an untapped opportunity for us. So, I created a plan to engage a wider audience across two social media platforms and to develop an annual impact report. The report expanded our reach by providing updates to those already on our mailing list, while social media allowed us to introduce our work to new audiences. Both strategies proved highly effective in increasing awareness and strengthening our connection with the community.

How Are You Sharing Your Organization's Story?

Are you highlighting the beneficiaries of your work? Do your donors and supporters understand the impact of their contributions? If you want to be more strategic with storytelling, it starts by clarifying your purpose, centering the people you serve, and using a blend of data and real-life experiences.

Start with a Clear Purpose

Before beginning any type of storytelling—whether written, visual, or verbal—be clear about what you hope to achieve. Are you trying to increase volunteer sign-ups, attract donors, or raise awareness about a specific issue?

For example, if you lead an after-school program and want to sell tickets for a fundraising event, focus your story on the impact attendees' support will have. Share how the event will benefit your mission and highlight the people it supports. You might craft a message like this for social media:

"When Ashley joined our mentorship program, she was struggling in school and lacked confidence in her STEM courses. Her mom had even hired a tutor, but Ashley didn't connect with them. Through weekly sessions with her mentor, she discovered her passion for engineering and is now excelling in all STEM classes at her high school. This gala will help fund opportunities for more students like Ashley to participate in our yearlong mentoring program. One ticket

purchase directly covers the cost of one week of snacks for one student in the program."

Along with this post, you could include a photo of Ashley with her mentor or a short video of them working together. This story is purposeful—it clearly communicates the event's goal (to sell more tickets) and connects attendees to the real impact of their support. By defining your desired outcome, you can craft-focused, relevant narratives that drive action.

Center the Human Element

Nothing resonates more than real stories that reflect genuine human experiences. People are far more likely to support a cause when they can see the individuals whose lives have been transformed by your work.

To center the human element in your storytelling, highlight the voices of those you serve, your volunteers, or your staff. You might:

▸ **Post a short video** of a volunteer sharing why they got involved and what the experience has meant to them.

▸ **Host a "Meet Our Team" series** on social media, spotlighting staff members and their personal stories.

▸ **Organize a panel discussion** where beneficiaries share how your programs have impacted their lives.

Each of these approaches puts the focus on the people behind your mission. Use anecdotes, interviews, or case studies that illustrate not just *what* your organization does, but *why* it matters. As leaders, we often understand our organization's purpose deeply, but it's vital to communicate that purpose in a way others can connect with. By telling stories that provide context and emotion, you invite people to become part of your mission.

Incorporate Both Data and Emotion

Think about the last movie that made you tear up or left you reflecting long after the credits rolled. Maybe you connected with a particular character's story, or maybe a powerful monologue stayed with you. What you experienced was an emotional connection—something that great storytelling achieves.

Are you applying this same approach in how you share your organization's work?

Earlier in this book, we discussed the importance of being data-informed. While data is crucial for making informed decisions and building credibility, it's equally important to pair it with compelling narratives. A story grounded in data provides both factual credibility and emotional appeal, striking a balance that helps audiences connect with—and believe in—your mission.

For example, a nonprofit working to end homelessness might share the following story in their annual report:

"Nearly half of households in this city can't meet the $55K/year cost for a 2-bedroom apartment, leaving many vulnerable to eviction and homelessness. With 35% of our unhoused population living without shelter and affordable housing options dwindling, the crisis is urgent. That's why

our mission is vital—providing shelter, support, and a pathway to lasting stability."

This narrative combines hard data with a community need, showing both the scale of the problem and the tangible impact of your organization's work. When you intertwine data with storytelling, you inspire confidence while fostering empathy, motivating your audience to take action.

Storytelling isn't just about explaining what you do—it's about showing your work in a way that invites people to form a connection. Reflect on the channels your organization is currently using and explore ways to better share your impact with a wider audience.

Remember: When you share your mission through authentic, relatable narratives, you create emotional connections that data alone can't achieve. Use storytelling to showcase your impact, build trust, and inspire others to join your journey.

PART 4

Sustaining Success

" *Sustainable leadership begins with resilience, adaptability, and care for self and others. Lasting impact requires us to lead with intention and evolve with purpose.*"

Visit www.myleadershipbook.com to download the Adaptive Leadership Plan.

CHAPTER 9

Practice Self-Care

"Self-care isn't an indulgence; it's the foundation of sustainable leadership."

I saved this topic for near the end of the book because, honestly, it's probably the most challenging one for me as a nonprofit leader. Despite earning multiple degrees, accumulating certifications, and receiving awards for my work, self-care wasn't something I had mastered. I knew how to set goals and achieve them. Even when things got tough, I could reach out for support, research until I found an answer, or problem-solve my way to a solution. My work ethic was solid—and I'm sure your story is similar.

I know many nonprofit leaders who regularly put in 60-hour workweeks and spend their weekends catching up on emails. They take work home, answering messages while sitting on the couch, watching their kids play after dinner. I don't underestimate the level of commitment and effort you're willing to put in. But the one area where I struggled for years—and still occasionally do—is how I approach my self-care and overall well-being.

Over the past decade, self-care has become something of a buzzword. What immediately came to mind for me were expensive yoga classes, green smoothies, and spa days filled with massages and facials. I equated self-care with something costly, time-consuming, and often impractical. I imagined needing to take entire days off work just to engage in "proper" self-care. And, of course, in our social media-driven world, the idea seemed tied to curated photos of people flaunting their self-care routines—complete with captions about mindfulness and wellness.

What I quickly realized, though, is that while self-care *can* include those things, at its core, it's simply about taking intentional steps to care for your physical, mental, and emotional health. The issue is that much of what we see and hear about self-care has been commercialized—designed to sell products or experiences. No wonder so many people feel like real self-care is out of reach.

When I first tried to "take care of myself," I followed the commercialized script. I took time off work, overspent on activities and products I thought would help, and quickly discovered that this approach wasn't sustainable. True self-care doesn't have to be expensive or time-consuming. In fact, making self-care accessible and sustainable is key to ensuring it becomes a regular part of your life.

Redefining Self-Care for Leaders

As nonprofit leaders, we're no strangers to hard work. Many of us could probably write a book on how to cram a thousand tasks into five minutes. But when it comes to taking care of ourselves, many of us are complete strangers to the concept. Each day, I see a new study about exhaustion or stress that highlights the overwhelming feeling felt by nonprofit leaders across the nation. Leaders are choosing to prioritize their workplace's goals and mission over their wellbeing, and it's causing burnout.

If you're reading this book, you might fall into that group of leaders who are burned out from doing mission-critical work. I get it—we can raise the funds, write the reports, and host all the events, but if we're not around to see the long-term impact of our work, then what's the point? We *must* take care of ourselves. I know that's easier said than done, but if we don't prioritize our well-being, we simply won't last in this field.

This chapter isn't about telling you to sign up for a gym membership or start exercising four days a week. Instead, it's about helping you reflect on what wellness and self-care mean to *you* and how you can integrate small, manageable moments of self-care into your daily routine. Because if you only take care of yourself on weekends or during the two weeks of vacation, you allow yourself each year, you're setting yourself up for burnout.

The Pressure to Prove Yourself

For many of us, the struggle with self-care starts with the pressure to prove ourselves. When I became an Executive Director, a few people openly questioned my qualifications. In fact, some longtime supporters of the organization looked me in the eye and said, "We don't really have a lot of confidence in you, but we do hope you do well."

With that kind of reception, I felt an immediate need to prove myself. I wanted to prove everyone wrong—the people who doubted me, the supporters who questioned the board's decision to hire me, and even those who were silently skeptical. I worked tirelessly, driven by a desire to validate my position and show that I was capable.

Long hours became the norm. On days when committee meetings ran late, I often worked 12-hour shifts, staying at the office until eight in the evening. I even missed dinner with my family a few times while scrambling to meet a grant application deadline. My first real lesson in self-care came after I literally crashed and burned out.

Two years into my role, I sat at my desk and felt a sudden tightness in my chest. I brushed it off—I was in my twenties, after all. Surely, nothing serious could be happening. But the discomfort didn't go away. Three hours later, reluctantly, I drove myself to a nearby urgent care center. Fortunately, the EKG didn't show signs of a heart attack, but the physician quickly pointed out that my work habits were taking a toll on my health. Besides the chest pains, I had frequent tension headaches, lived on coffee, and couldn't remember the last time I ate a full meal without multitasking.

My life revolved entirely around the organization. Even when I wasn't physically at the office, my mind was consumed with work—planning meetings, drafting agendas, conducting donor research. Weekends weren't for relaxation; they were for getting ahead on the next week's tasks.

My passion for self-care stems from this personal experience. I believe deeply in the work you do, and I also believe you can do it without sacrificing your health. Before I share some self-care strategies that go beyond the usual advice to "eat healthy and exercise," I want you to experience a brief moment of self-care right now. Let's pause:

1. Put this book (or device) down.
2. Stand up—yes, really, stand up—and stretch your arms as high as you can.
3. Close your eyes and take one slow, deliberate breath: inhale for four seconds, hold, then exhale for four seconds.

Congratulations! You just carved out space for yourself in a day likely packed with responsibilities. It might feel a little silly, but incorporating mini-pauses like this can lead to noticeable change. Now that we're on the same page (pun intended), let's dive into three practical strategies you can implement right away. I'm not going to tell you to hit the gym at 5 a.m. or buy kale in bulk. Instead, think of each strategy as a simple experiment you can try this week, even if it's only for a few minutes.

Practice Boundary-Setting

Boundaries are fundamental—they protect your health and well-being by helping you say "no" to things that threaten your commitments to yourself. Setting boundaries allows you to focus on what matters most, enabling you to do your best work without being pulled in every direction. Reflecting on my leadership journey, I can trace many of my most stressful moments to times when I didn't know how to say "no."

As a leader, people constantly look to you to "do" things for them. Whether it's a donor, a volunteer, or a staff member, you're likely juggling too many tasks with not enough time. That's why it's critical to establish boundaries around your time. If you're unsure where to start, here are a few tips:

▸ **Keep a short daily "No" list.** Each day, write down one or two things you will say "no" to—such as an extra meeting request or checking emails late at night. Put a sticky note on your desk or phone as a visual reminder to enforce that boundary.

▸ **Block time for mini-breaks.** Schedule even 15-minute chunks where you're off-limits—no phone, no emails, no interruptions. Use that time to breathe, stretch, or do something non-work-related.

▸ **Prioritize non-negotiables.** Identify parts of your schedule that are sacred, such as dinner with family or a weekly hour for personal development and treat those appointments as you would a donor meeting.

Boundaries not only protect your well-being but also communicate to others how you value your time. Take a look at your current calendar and identify areas where you could fine-tune your boundaries.

Schedule Small Mindful Moments

I used to believe rest was something you earned on vacation or during an organization-wide holiday. I held my breath between these rare breaks, hoping they would keep me going. But waiting for big breaks to recharge only kept me in a constant cycle of burnout. Eventually, I realized that just as overwork adds up, so do small moments of rest.

You already experienced a mindful moment at the start of this chapter—now imagine building those moments into your routine throughout the day. Even setting a timer or using an app to remind you to pause, breathe, or stretch can help. Here are a few ideas for mindful moments you can easily incorporate into your workday:

▸ **Do a posture check.** Sit up straight, roll your shoulders back, lift your chin slightly, and imagine a string pulling you upward from the top of your head. If you spend a lot of time at a desk, this quick adjustment can relieve tension.

▸ **Take a timed pause.** Set a timer for 1–2 minutes and spend that time doing absolutely nothing related to work—no emails, no phone calls, no social media.

▸ **Create a short playlist.** Pick a few songs that energize or calm you. When you need a break, listen to 30 seconds of a song, close your eyes, and enjoy the music without multitasking.

Hold yourself accountable by checking in at the end of each day: "What felt good today? What felt overwhelming?" Even if you only take a minute to pause, that's progress. Start small and build from there.

Make Space for Personal Creativity

When was the last time you allowed yourself to be creative during the workday? Engaging in creative activities—even briefly—can give your brain a break from productivity-driven thinking, spark new ideas, and provide a refreshing shift in perspective.

One of my favorite memories from a leadership conference was being given an adult coloring book at registration. I hadn't colored in years, and I'd forgotten how much fun it could be. That experience reminded me of the joy I felt as a child when I ran, danced, sang loudly, or painted. While I don't consider myself an artist, those moments gave me a sense of freedom and left me feeling refreshed—something we could all use more of.

If you want to add creativity to your routine, here are some simple ideas:

▸ **Change your environment.** Work in a different room, head outside or visit a café to stimulate new ideas.

▸ **Use creative tools for brainstorming.** Instead of writing ideas in a plain document, use colorful markers, sticky notes, or mind-mapping software.

▸ **Swap mindless scrolling for creative play.** Instead of scrolling through emails or social media between meetings, listen to an inspiring podcast, jot down fundraising ideas, or doodle in a notebook.

Even one creative activity can spark innovation and offer a new perspective. Don't be afraid to try something new—it might just refresh your thinking.

Sustainable Self-Care Happens in Small Steps

It's easy to feel like there's never enough time for self-care, but as we've explored, small changes—like setting boundaries, taking mindful breaks, and allowing space for creativity—can make a significant difference. Sustainable self-care happens in daily, bite-sized moments: a few intentional breaths between meetings, a quick journal entry at lunch, or a firm "no" when your plate is already full.

Remember: You can't pour from an empty cup. Prioritizing your well-being ensures that you can lead with energy, clarity, and purpose.

CHAPTER 10

Embrace Adaptive Leadership

❝ *In a world of constant change, the best leaders evolve while staying rooted in their mission."*

Without question, the most unexpected challenge I've ever faced as a leader was navigating the COVID-19 pandemic in 2020. A global pandemic certainly wasn't on my list of potential challenges, and everything I did in the years that followed became a process of trial and error.

I still recall sitting at my desk when I first heard reports of COVID-19 cases in my area. Initially, I wasn't sure how to proceed—until the statewide mandate came, requiring students to transition to virtual learning. Soon after, local businesses began announcing closures, and organizations scrambled to shift to remote work.

Fortunately, just a few months earlier, our board had voted to take the organization fully remote and move out of our physical office space. Over the prior 90 days, I had focused on transitioning our team to remote operations. I had no way of knowing a global pandemic was on the horizon, but to this day, it stands as one of my proudest accomplishments. By the time shutdowns began, we already had virtual meeting systems in place, and everyone was equipped to work from home. The solid infrastructure we built allowed us to shift many of our programs online with minimal disruption.

However, the challenges brought on by the pandemic extended far beyond remote work. One of the biggest hurdles we encountered was the cancellation of our annual fundraiser, which typically accounted for a quarter of our yearly revenue. With that large source of funding gone, we had to pivot quickly—applying for emergency grants to offset the loss. I spent much of 2020 preoccupied with our financial sustainability, grappling with a crisis for which none of us had a roadmap. I joined Facebook groups, consulted experts, and scoured the internet for solutions—but often came up empty-handed. It was uncharted territory, and I had no choice but to build the plane while flying it.

While we successfully hosted many of our core workshops online, we couldn't ignore the emotional toll the pandemic took on our participants. Many were dealing with loss, anxiety, and frustration. We adjusted our programming to be more responsive to their emotional needs, offering not only education but also a space for empathy and support. Internally, our team faced its own set of challenges. With schools closed, many staff members were juggling childcare while working remotely. This added complexity required us to offer greater flexibility and understanding.

One of the most important lessons I took from that experience was the value of agility and flexibility. I had always heard that nonprofit leaders must be prepared for the unexpected, but I never imagined how true that would become. The pandemic underscored the importance of adaptability and resilience—skills I continue to prioritize today. I learned that while having a detailed plan is ideal, it's equally vital to create space for agility so you can respond effectively when things don't go as planned.

When thinking about your organization's agility, ask yourself: how are you fostering a culture that enables your team, board, and volunteers to remain adaptive? While a global pandemic is an extreme example, challenges requiring innovation and quick adjustment are common. Economic downturns, changes in donor behavior, leadership transitions, and evolving community needs can all test an organization's ability to pivot. Without a culture of adaptability, your organization risks instability and missed opportunities. An adaptive organization is one that anticipates change, prepares for it, and knows how to pivot when necessary. This requires transparent communication, a willingness to innovate, and a commitment to resilience at every level.

Cultivate a Learning Mindset

In the chapter on team development, I discussed fostering a learning culture. That mindset also applies to how you approach challenges. Consider how you can create an environment where both you and your team view obstacles as opportunities to learn and grow. Part of fostering a learning culture involves seeking regular feedback from your team and stakeholders. This feedback is essential for identifying what's working, what isn't, and where adjustments are needed. Ensure that there's a continuous feedback loop to support ongoing improvement.

Staying informed about sector trends is another key component of adaptability. For example, if you work in the food justice sector, are you up to date on legislation affecting food access in your region? Are you tracking national trends that could impact local funding or policies? During my time leading an education-focused organization, I closely monitored local, state, and national conversations about education to ensure our program was prepared for potential changes.

Scenario Planning

Scenario planning is a proactive way to prepare for the "what ifs." This doesn't mean obsessing over worst-case scenarios but rather considering a range of possibilities so you're ready to respond effectively. Whether it's a significant funding cut, a sudden leadership transition, or an unexpected community need, scenario planning equips your organization to remain proactive rather than reactive.

Start by identifying potential disruptions that could impact your organization's work. These might include economic fluctuations, shifts in donor priorities, policy changes, or internal factors like staff turnover. For each scenario, develop at least two potential responses: one for an ideal outcome where everything aligns perfectly and another as a fallback plan in case things don't go as expected. Ask yourself: What resources would we need? Who should be involved in our response? What steps can we take today to reduce risks and avoid being caught off guard? This approach helps create a flexible framework that positions your organization to pivot when needed.

In addition, scenario planning is an excellent team-building exercise. Engaging your team, board, and key stakeholders in these discussions often sparks creativity and strengthens collaboration. These conversations can reveal blind spots and uncover opportunities you may not have previously considered. Even if the scenarios you plan for never happen, you've strengthened your organization's capacity to adapt. And when the unexpected inevitably does arise, you'll have the clarity, confidence, and structure to respond effectively—instead of scrambling for solutions in the moment.

Simplify Processes for Faster Responses

Streamlining processes is about simplifying how your organization operates so you can work smarter, not harder. It's common for nonprofits to continue using outdated methods simply because "that's how things have always been done." But by stepping back to examine your workflows, you can uncover where time, energy, and resources are being wasted—and design systems that enable your team to achieve more with less effort.

Take donor acknowledgments, for example. Suppose your organization currently handles this manually: after receiving a donation, a staff member writes a personalized thank-you note, prints it, addresses an envelope, and mails it. While personal touches matter, this process can be simplified without sacrificing impact. By using donor management software, you could automate thank-you emails to be sent immediately after a gift is received, complete with personalized details such as the donor's name and contribution amount. For major donors, you might still send handwritten notes, but automation ensures that every donor is promptly acknowledged. This revised system saves hours of staff time while maintaining strong donor relationships and demonstrating gratitude efficiently.

When processes are clear and streamlined, you reduce frustration and free up mental energy for more creative, strategic work. Consistent systems also mean that whether someone is new to your team or a long-time staff member, they can follow established, reliable processes with ease.

Embrace Iteration Over Perfection

I saved the best for last because, as a recovering perfectionist, this lesson has been invaluable for me. I've often found myself caught in endless cycles of reviewing and brainstorming, waiting for something to be "just right" before moving forward. In nonprofit leadership, however, the pursuit of perfection can be paralyzing. It delays progress, increases pressure, and keeps you from seizing opportunities. Instead of striving for perfection, focus on iteration—making small, continuous improvements as you go. This approach allows you to innovate in real time rather than waiting for an ideal solution before taking action.

For instance, if you're launching a new community initiative, start with a pilot group or a limited audience. Use their feedback to refine your approach before scaling up. This strategy reduces risk, builds trust with your team and stakeholders, and generates valuable data and insights to guide future improvements. In short, you get to enhance your work as you build.

When you embrace iteration as a leader, it creates a ripple effect across your organization. Your team will feel empowered to propose new ideas without waiting for the "perfect" solution. They'll adopt a mindset of experimentation, seeing challenges as opportunities to innovate rather than obstacles to avoid. This culture of learning strengthens your team, encouraging creativity and adaptability at every level.

As you reflect on this chapter, think about how you can become a more adaptive leader. Is there a program you've been delaying that could start as a pilot project? Are there outdated processes that need to be reviewed and updated? Or maybe it's as simple as viewing each daily challenge as a chance to learn and grow your leadership skills.

Remember: Change is inevitable, but adaptability is your greatest strength. Approach challenges with a mindset of innovation and continuous improvement and lead your organization confidently into the future.

EPILOGUE

Now that you've completed this book, you have the strategies needed to move forward in your leadership journey with confidence and clarity. I hope that these lessons serve as guideposts, helping you lead with resilience and create meaningful impact. Don't let this book gather dust on your shelf—share it with a colleague or friend who might benefit from its insights. Let it become a resource you revisit throughout your leadership journey.

Above all, I hope you believe in your ability to lead and in your organization's potential to drive lasting change. Know that you have what it takes to build a sustainable, successful organization. Keep taking small, intentional steps toward realizing your vision and making a difference for future generations. Remember, leadership isn't about having all the answers—it's about being willing to keep learning.

As a reminder, here are the ten key strategies we covered:

1. **Understand Your Ecosystem:** Start with the big picture. Familiarize yourself with the environment, stakeholders, and interconnected systems that influence your organization.
2. **Know Your Data:** Get comfortable with the numbers. Data-driven decisions are crucial for

guiding your strategy and achieving your mission.

3. **Master Financial Literacy:** Strengthen your organization's foundation by effectively managing budgets, revenue streams, and financial planning.

4. **Cultivate Donor Relationships:** Focus on building genuine connections with donors by aligning their passions with your organization's goals. Relationships, not transactions, drive long-term support.

5. **Leverage Community Partnerships:** Collaborate with community partners who share your vision. Working together amplifies your impact and broadens your reach.

6. **Strengthen Board Engagement:** Align your board around a shared vision. Treat them as partners in advancing your mission and empower them to become advocates for your work.

7. **Develop Your Team:** Invest in your team's growth and create a culture of shared leadership. Empowering others ensures long-term sustainability.

8. **Tell Your Story Strategically:** Use storytelling to inspire action. Craft compelling narratives that connect with your audience and highlight your organization's mission and achievements.

9. **Practice Self-Care:** Prioritize your well-being by setting boundaries and protecting your energy. A healthy, balanced leader is better equipped to lead effectively.

10. **Embrace Adaptive Leadership:** Stay flexible and open to change. Lead with creativity and courage, remaining anchored in your mission while navigating uncertainty.

These strategies are not just theoretical concepts—they are actionable steps you can implement to lead with greater confidence, adaptability, and purpose. As you've seen through the stories and lessons shared in this book, leadership requires both grit and grace. It's about staying focused on your mission while embracing growth and continuous learning. There's always more to learn, and that's what makes leadership a lifelong journey. I invite you to visit www.myleadership-book.com for additional resources that will help you unpack the strategies shared in this book.

If you need support along your leadership journey, reach out to me via www.tamaradias.com for information on the Nonprofit Leadership Coaching Program. I also provide facilitation for workshops and retreats for nonprofit organizations and boards of directors. You don't have to navigate this journey alone, and I am here to support you!

Over time, your leadership path will evolve, bringing new challenges and opportunities. Carry these strategies with you as a roadmap and always remember that your work matters. Your impact goes beyond your organization—it shapes the communities and lives you serve.

Thank you for taking this journey with me. Now, it's time to put what you've learned into action and lead boldly into the future.

ABOUT THE AUTHOR

Dr. Tamara W. Dias is a dynamic leader with over a decade of experience driving meaningful change across both nonprofit and corporate sectors. She specializes in aligning organizational goals with innovative strategies that promote learning, leadership development, and long-term sustainability. As Executive Director of an education-focused nonprofit, Dr. Dias led a remarkable transformation, doubling program enrollment while streamlining operations to achieve significant cost savings. Her unwavering commitment to equity and inclusion is evident in the comprehensive employee engagement initiatives she developed, which have enhanced both staff satisfaction and retention.

Beyond her executive leadership role, Dr. Dias is a sought-after coach, consultant, and speaker. Through her coaching practice, she empowers nonprofit leaders and executives to overcome challenges, build resilience, and foster sustainable impact within their organizations. With a focus on leadership development, board governance, and strategic advising, Dr. Dias customizes her approach to meet the unique needs of mission-driven organizations. Her consulting work has benefited nonprofits of varying sizes, particularly those with budgets under $5 million, helping them navigate resource constraints and achieve their goals with creativity and integrity. As a speaker, she captivates audiences with insightful, actionable perspectives on key topics such as nonprofit leadership sustainability, diversity and inclusion, and equity-driven mission work.

Dr. Dias partners with nonprofits through her consulting firm to create strategic plans, strengthen board governance, and cultivate leadership excellence. Her tailored approach equips leaders with practical tools to navigate complex challenges, align organizational actions with mission goals, and drive lasting change. Renowned for her ability to transform ambitious visions into actionable strategies, Dr. Dias is a trusted advisor to nonprofits seeking to expand their capacity and deepen their community impact.

Dr. Dias is an engaging and thoughtful speaker known for delivering practical, results-driven insights on nonprofit leadership, sustainability, and strategic planning. Her presentations inspire nonprofit leaders to move beyond immediate obstacles and focus on building a foundation for long-term success.

Dr. Dias is a dedicated servant leader who has shared her expertise by serving on numerous boards, including the Virginia African American Advisory Board and Women United in Philanthropy. She holds a Doctor of Education in Leadership from Morgan State University and is widely celebrated for her ability to create systemic, meaningful change. Additionally, she earned a Master of Teaching in Foreign Language Education and a Bachelor of Arts in Spanish Linguistics and Philology from the University of Virginia. Dr. Dias also holds certifications in Adult Learning and Development, Behavioral Consulting, and Diversity, Equity, and Inclusion—further solidifying her reputation as a trusted expert and advocate for organizational growth and equity.